In Your Fifties and Still Got It!

THIS IS A PRION BOOK

First published in Great Britain in 2016 by Prion
An imprint of the Carlton Publishing Group
20 Mortimer Street
London W1T 3JW

A CIP catalogue for this book is available from the British Library.

ISBN 978-1-85375-956-7

Printed in Dubai

10 9 8 7 6 5 4 3 2 1

In Your Fifties and Still Got It!

Humorous and Inspirational Quotes for those Aged 50 and Beyond

PRION

Contents

Introduction

You deserve a well-earned break. But don't sit down for too long as you may never get up again. Just kidding.

Now, as depressing as being 50+ looks when you see yourself in the mirror, just remember that getting this far in life is a major achievement, no matter what your children may think. From here on in, it's all plain sailing.

So, throw away your slippers, say 'no' to those pointless quiz shows and blow away the cobwebs that are forming in your head… it's time to say yes to buying that speedboat! You're 50 and still rocking, so turn the music up and get on down, it's time to party… until 9.30pm, at least. Enjoy!

Fifty Shades of Grey

"Whatever poet, orator or sage may say of it, old age is still old age."

Sinclair Lewis

"One starts to get young at the age of 60."

Pablo Picasso

"Looking 50 is great... if you're 60."

Joan Rivers

"Forty is the old age of youth;
50 the youth of old age."

Victor Hugo

"I'm aiming by the time I'm 50
to stop being an adolescent."

Wendy Cope

"Nature gives you the face you have
at 20; it is up to you to merit the
face you have at 50."

Coco Chanel

"At 20 a man is a peacock,
at 30 a lion, at 40 a camel,
at 50 a serpent, at 60 a dog,
at 70 an ape,
at 80 a nothing at all."

Baltasar Gracian

"I have enjoyed greatly the second blooming... suddenly you find at the age of 50, say, that a whole new life has opened before you."

Agatha Christie

"At 50, everyone has the face he deserves."

George Orwell

"A man who views the world the same at 50 as he did at 20 has wasted 30 years of his life."

Muhammad Ali

"At 50 confine your piercings to sardine cans."

Joan Rivers

"People under 34 think old age starts around 55. Those over 75, on the other hand, believe that youth doesn't end until the age of 58."

Alexander Chancellor

"Except ye become as little children, except you can wake on your 50th birthday with the same forward looking excitement and interest in life that you enjoyed when you were five, "ye cannot enter the kingdom of God." One must not only die daily, but every day we must be born again."

Dorothy L. Sayers

"I'm 59 and people call me middle-aged. How many 118-year-old men do you know?"

Barry Cryer

"At 50, you have the choice of keeping your face or your figure and it's much better to keep your face."

Barbara Cartland

"Every businessman over 50 should have a daily nap and nip; a short nap after lunch and a relaxing highball before dinner."

Dr. Sara Murray Jordan

"I'm 57. I can't look like a 30-year-old. You try to hold age at bay, but there comes a point when you just have to give up gracefully."

Elton John

"My 50 years have shown me that few people know what they are talking about. I don't mean idiots that don't know. I mean everyone."

John Cleese

"When men reach their sixties and retire they go to pieces. Women just go right on cooking."

Gail Sheehy

"On my 50th birthday my wife gave me a superb birthday present. She let me win an argument."

Anon

"I think when the full horror of being 50 hits you, you should stay home and have a good cry."

Alan Bleasdale

"When your friends begin to flatter you on how young you look, it's a sure sign you're getting old."

Mark Twain

"I have been a woman for 50 years, and I've never yet been able to discover precisely what it is I am."

Jean Giraudoux

"I think middle age is the best time, if we can escape the fatty degeneration of the conscience which often sets in at about 50."

William Ralph Inge

"By the time we hit 50, we have learned our hardest lessons. We have found out that only a few things are really important. We have learned to take life seriously, but never ourselves."

Marie Dressler

"The real sadness of 50 is not that you change so much but that you change so little."

Max Lerner

"I keep telling people I'll make movies until I'm 50 and then I'll go and do something else. I'm going to be a professional gentleman of leisure."

Eddie Murphy

"What a man knows at 50 that he did not know at 20 is for the most part incommunicable."

Adlai E. Stevenson

"50 is the new 40. I always thought my best work would come in the years 40 to 60, if I was fortunate enough to hang around and it is hard to stick around."

Bruce Willis

"You may be sick of what you did the first half of your life, but you don't have to just walk around and play golf or doing nothing. It's not like 50 is the new 30. It's like 50 is the new chapter."

Sharon Stone

"At 50, that is in 1880, I formulated the idea of unity, without being able to render it. At 60, I am beginning to see the possibility of rendering it."

Camille Pissarro

"By the age of 50, you have made yourself what you are, and if it is good, it is better than your youth."

Marya Mannes

"Sex is as good at 50 as it was at 20. The only difference is I'm not into all that freakin' Cirque de Soleil stuff because I'm as flexible as a two-by-four with as much stamina as an emphysema patient on oxygen."

Janet Periat

"After 50, one ceases to digest. As someone once said, I just ferment my food now."

Henry Green

"For my 50th birthday, my husband and I spent a weekend in Rehoboth Beach. My first choice was 1978, but the time-machine was booked."

Jean Sorensen

"Celebrating 50 is like throwing a party when your odometer reaches 150,000 miles."

Melanie White

"At 21 you're finally free to slam down the throttle and see how fast you can go. At 30 you realize, hey, this thing has a brake pedal too. By 40, that brake pedal is showing some serious wear. At 50, let's face it, you need a brake job."

Greg Tamblyn

"Fifty years old? Look on the bright side. The older you get, the more likely you are to outlive your child support payments."

Melanie White

"Fifty years old means no more wearing speedos on the beach. This is a rule."

Greg Tamblyn

"Fifty years: here's a time when you have to separate yourself from what other people expect of you, and do what you love. Because if you find yourself 50 years old and you aren't doing what you love, then what's the point?"

Jim Carrey

"At 50, you've entered the stone age: gall, kidney, and bladder."

Anon

"The worst thing anyone has ever said about me is that I'm 50. Which I am. Oh that bitch. I was so hurt."

Joan Rivers

"At age 20, we worry about what others think of us. At age 40, we don't care what they think of us. At age 60, we discover they haven't been thinking of us at all."

Ann Landers

"Whenever the talk turns to age,
I say I am 49 plus VAT."

Lionel Blair

"It seems that after the age of 50, I began to age at the rate of about three years per year. I began falling asleep 15 minutes into an episode of *Seinfeld*. I also began falling asleep during sex rather than after."

Anon

"If you haven't grown up by age 50,
you don't have to."

Anon

"I don't believe that when you
are 25 you are over the hill.
Fifty is the new 30."

Michael Flatley

"You take all of the experience and judgment of men over 50 out of the world and there wouldn't be enough left to run it."

Henry Ford

"Every woman over 50 should stay in bed until noon."

Mamie Eisenhower

"The heyday of a woman's life is the shady side of 50."

Elizabeth Cady Stanton

"Time wounds all heels."

Groucho Marx

"Your fifties are mature, reliable and dependable, or boring, predictable and conventional."

T. Kinnes

"One has to be able to count if only so that at 50 one doesn't marry a girl of 20."

Maxim Gorky

"When you get to 52 food becomes more important than sex."

Prue Leith

"You know you're 50 when you're in an elevator when your favorite song comes on."

Anon

The Golden Age

"The golden age is before us, not behind us."

William Shakespeare

"The great thing about getting older is that you don't lose all the other ages you've been."

Madeleine L'Engle

"Hey, even the Mona Lisa is falling apart."

Chuck Palahniuk

"The years between 50 and 70 are the hardest. You are always being asked to do more, and you are not yet decrepit enough to turn them down."

T. S. Eliot

"I'm only two years older than Brad Pitt, but I look a lot older, which used to greatly frustrate me. It doesn't any more."

George Clooney

"After a man passes 60, his mischief is mainly in his head."

Washington Irving

"Now that I think of it, I wish I had been a hellraiser when I was 30 years old. I tried it when I was 50 but I always got sleepy."

Groucho Marx

"A man is a fool if he drinks before he reaches the age of 50, and a fool if he doesn't afterward."

Frank Lloyd Wright

"I've got all the money I'll ever need if I die by four o'clock this afternoon."

Henny Youngman

"I drive with my knees. Otherwise, how can I put on my lipstick and talk on my phone?"

Sharon Stone

"My memory is going. I brush my teeth, and then ten minutes later I go back and have to feel the toothbrush. Is it wet? Did I just brush them?"

Terry Gilliam

"I can see nothing wrong with 40-, 50-, or 60-year-old men dressing and acting like men. I'm an elderly man and, after a few miserable years of being sensible, I do it all the time."

Jeremy Clarkson

"You're not drunk if you can lie on the floor without holding on."

Joe E. Lewis

"Sex is a bad thing because it rumples the clothes."

Jackie Onassis

"Thank God! Now I realize I've been chained to an idiot for the last 60 years of my life!"

Kingsley Amis, on his lost libido

"The worst thing a man can do is go bald. Never let yourself go bald."

Donald Trump

"My formula for living is quite simple. I get up in the morning and I go to bed at night. In between, I occupy myself as best I can."

Cary Grant

"A 90-year-old man was asked to what he attributed his longevity. 'I reckon,' he said, with a twinkle in his eye, 'it's because most nights I went to bed and slept when I should have sat up and worried.'"

Dorothea Kent

"We must always change, renew, rejuvenate ourselves; otherwise we harden."

Johann Wolfgang Goethe

"You can't have everything.
Where would you put it?"

Steven Wright

"I've had to tone it down a bit. But I've still got fabulous legs and wear miniskirts. I'll keep wearing bikinis until I'm 80... I will grow old gracefully in public and disgracefully in private."

Jerry Hall

"If you obey all the rules,
you miss all the fun."

Katharine Hepburn

"Men become old, but they never
become good. As men get older,
their toys get more expensive."

Oscar Wilde

"If you can't have fun as an ageing sex symbol when you hit 60, I don't know what will become of you."

Raquel Welch

"The pleasures that once were heaven, look silly at 67."

Noel Coward

"My wife Mary and I have been married for 47 years and not once have we had an argument serious enough to consider divorce; murder, yes, but divorce, never."

Jack Benny

"There is a fountain of youth: it is your mind, your talents, the creativity you bring to your life and the lives of the people you love. When you learn to tap this source, you will have truly defeated age."

Sophia Loren

"Time flies like an arrow. Fruit flies like a banana."

Groucho Marx

"There are only two ways to live your life. One is as though nothing is a miracle. The other is as though everything is a miracle."

Albert Einstein

"If you survive long enough, you're revered rather like an old building."

Katherine Hepburn

"We grow too soon old and
too late smart."

Dutch proverb

"I love everything that's old:
old friends, old times, old manners,
old books, old wines."

Oliver Goldsmith

"You will recognize, my boy, the first sign of old age: it is when you go out into the streets of London and realize for the first time how young the policemen look."

Sir Seymour Hicks

"A woman is like a tea bag; you never know how strong it is until it's in hot water."

Eleanor Roosevelt

"I have learned that to be with those I like is enough."

Walt Whitman

"Never lose sight of the fact that old age needs so little but needs that little so much."

Margaret Willour

"I don't want to die an old lady."

Edith Piaf

"Life is a moderately good play with a badly written third act."

Truman Capote

"No woman ever ages beyond 18 in her heart."

Robert A. Heinlein

"And in the end, it's not the years in your life that count. It's the life in your years."

Abraham Lincoln

"It's so hard when you're young to look at older people and understand that they have been where you are. It's the weirdest thing. You just can't get your head around that, can you? You can't get your head around the fact that someone who is 60 was once 16, if you're 16. But the fact is they have been, and they remember it."

Helen Mirren

"To get back my youth I would do anything in the world, except take exercise, get up early or be respectable."

Oscar Wilde

"When people talk about the good old days, I say to people, 'It's not the days that are old, it's you that's old.' I hate the good old days. What is important is that today is good."

Karl Lagerfeld

"Just remember, when you're over the hill, you begin to pick up speed."

Charles M. Schulz

"If youth knew; if age could."

Henri Estienne

"I don't believe in ageing. I believe in forever altering one's aspect to the sun."

Virginia Woolf

"No woman should ever be quite accurate about her age. It looks so calculating."

Oscar Wilde

"I have reached an age when, if someone tells me to wear socks, I don't have to."

Albert Einstein

"The age of a woman doesn't mean a thing. The best tunes are played on the oldest fiddles."

Ralph Waldo Emerson

"Old age is no place for sissies."

Bette Davis

"Better pass boldly into that other world, in the full glory of some passion, than fade and wither dismally with age."

James Joyce

"Wives are young men's mistresses, companions for middle age, and old men's nurses."

Francis Bacon

"The older I grow, the more I distrust the familiar doctrine that age brings wisdom."

H. L. Mencken

"Youth has no age."

Pablo Picasso

"Setting a good example for your children takes all the fun out of middle age."

William Feather

"I think your whole life shows
in your face and you should
be proud of that."

Lauren Bacall

"It is sad to grow old
but nice to ripen."

Brigitte Bardot

"One starts to get young at the age
of 60 and then it is too late."

Pablo Picasso

"After 50 a man discovers he does not need more than one suit."

Clifton Fadiman

"I don't need you to remind me of my age. I have a bladder to do that for me."

Stephen Fry

"Be eccentric now. Don't wait for old age to wear purple."

Regina Brett

"Some day you will be old enough to start reading fairy tales again."

C. S. Lewis

"When you are dissatisfied and would like to go back to youth, think of algebra."

Will Rogers

"What is a younger woman? I'm pretty old, so almost every woman is younger than me."

Jack Nicholson

"Everything that goes up must come down. But there comes a time when not everything that's down can come up."

George Burns

"I usually take a two-hour nap from one to four."

Yogi Berra

"Try to keep your soul young and quivering right up to old age."

George Sand

Staying Alive

"Don't take life too seriously; you'll never get out of it alive."

Elbert Hubbard

"Jogging is for people who aren't intelligent enough to watch television."

Victoria Wood

"Who said there were no such things as miracles? You made it to 50, didn't you?"

Melanie White

"You can't turn back the clock.
But you can wind it up again."

Bonnie Prudden

"Maybe it's true that life begins
at 50. But everything else starts to
wear out, fall out or spread out."

Phyllis Diller

"I want to grow old without
facelifts. I want to have the courage
to be loyal to the face I have made."

Marilyn Monroe

"It's no longer a question of staying healthy. It's a question of finding a sickness you like."

Jackie Mason

"I buy all those celebrity exercise videos. I love to sit and eat cookies and watch them."

Dolly Parton

"I don't exercise. If God wanted me to bend over, he'd have put diamonds on the floor."

Joan Rivers

"If God wanted me to touch my toes, he would have put them on my knees."

Roseanne Barr

"The trouble with jogging is that by the time you realize you're not in shape for it, it's too far to walk back."

Franklin P. Jones

"I often take exercise. Only yesterday I had breakfast in bed."

Oscar Wilde

"In youth we run into difficulties. In old age difficulties run into us."

Beverly Sills

"First the doctor told me the good news: I was going to have a disease named after me."

Steve Martin

"I have finally come to the conclusion that a good reliable set of bowels is worth more to man than any quantity of brains."

Josh Billings

"I'm an old fashioned guy...
I want to be an old man with a
beer belly sitting on a porch,
looking at a lake or something."

Johnny Depp

"Sleep, those little slices of death,
how I loathe them."

Carrie Snow

"My husband said 'show me your
boobs' and I had to pull up my skirt...
so it was time to get them done!"

Dolly Parton

"I am pushing 60. That is enough exercise for me."

Mark Twain

"My idea of exercise is a good brisk sit."

Phyllis Diller

"One day you look in the mirror and you realize that the face you are shaving is your father's."

Robert Harris

"When I look in the mirror I don't see a rock star any more. I see a little balding old guy who looks like someone's uncle."

Pete Townshend

"Lack of activity destroys the good condition of every human being, while movement and methodical physical exercise save it and preserve it."

Plato

"Look at Cher. One more facelift and she'll be wearing a beard."

Jennifer Saunders

"Fitness – if it came in a bottle, everybody would have a great body."

Cher

"The word aerobics came about when the gym instructors got together and said, 'If we're going to charge $10 an hour, we can't call it jumping up and down.'"

Rita Rudner

"I have to exercise in the morning before my brain figures out what I'm doing."

Marsha Doble

"A bear, however hard he tries, grows tubby without exercise."

A. A. *Milne*

"You know you're getting fat when you can pinch an inch on your forehead."

John Mendoza

"I really don't think I need buns of steel. I'd be happy with buns of cinnamon."

Ellen DeGeneres

"Old age is a special problem for me because I've never been able to shed the mental image I have of myself – a lad of about 19."

E. B. White

"The youth of the present day are quite monstrous. They have absolutely no respect for dyed hair."

Oscar Wilde

"We are living in a world today where lemonade is made from artificial flavours and furniture polish is made from real lemons."

Alfred E. Newman

"You don't appreciate a lot of stuff in school until you get older. Little things like being spanked every day by a middle-aged woman: stuff you pay good money for in later life."

Emo Philips

"In a man's middle years there is scarcely a part of the body he would hesitate to turn over to the proper authorities."

E. B. White

"A man's age is something impressive, it sums up his life: maturity reached slowly and against many obstacles, illnesses cured, griefs and despairs overcome, and unconscious risks taken; maturity formed through so many desires, hopes, regrets, forgotten things, loves. A man's age represents a fine cargo of experiences and memories."

Antoine de Saint Exupéry

"Inflation is when you pay 15 dollars for the ten-dollar haircut you used to get for five dollars when you had hair."

Sam Ewing

"Live as long as you may, the first 20 years are the longest half of your life."

Robert Southey

"A man has reached middle age when he's warned to slow down by his doctor instead of the police."

Henry Youngman

"It is not all bad, this getting old, ripening. After the fruit has got its growth it should juice up and mellow. God forbid I should live long enough to ferment and rot and fall to the ground in a squash."

Emily Carr

"Sex appeal is 50% what you've got and 50% what people think you've got."

Sophia Loren

"When I was young, I was told: 'You'll see, when you're 50.' I am 50 and I haven't seen a thing."

Erik Satie

"Middle age is when your age starts to show around your middle."

Bob Hope

"You know you're 50 when the only silver lining you can see is on your head."

Melanie White

"Let us respect grey hairs,
especially our own."

J. P. Sears

"It's not that age brings childhood back again, age merely shows what children we remain."

Johann Wolfgang von Goethe

"It is after you have lost your teeth that you can afford to buy steaks."

Pierre-Auguste Renoir

"Do not go gentle into that good night... Rage, rage against the dying of the light."

Dylan Thomas

"Age only matters when one is ageing. Now that I have arrived at a great age, I might as well be 20."

Pablo Picasso

"The really frightening thing about middle age is the knowledge that you'll grow out of it."

Doris Day

"You can live to be a hundred if you give up all things that make you want to live to be a hundred."

Woody Allen

"Regular naps prevent old age, especially if you take them while driving."

Anon

"The face you have at age 25 is the face God gave you, but the face you have after 50 is the face you have earned."

Cindy Crawford

"Everything slows down with age, except the time it takes cake and ice cream to reach your hips."

John Wagner

"The secret of genius is to carry the spirit of the child into old age, which mean never losing your enthusiasm."

Aldous Huxley

"I don't know how you feel about old age... But in my case I didn't even see it coming. It hit me from the rear."

Phyllis Diller

"I drink too much. The last time I gave a urine sample it had an olive in it."

Rodney Dangerfield

"Everyone probably thinks that I'm a raving nymphomaniac, that I have an insatiable sexual appetite, when the truth is I'd rather read a book."

Madonna

"Middle age is having a choice of two temptations and choosing the one that will get you home earlier."

Dan Bennett

"Except for an occasional heart attack I feel as young as I ever did."

Robert Benchley

"You can add years to your life by wearing your pants backwards."

Johnny Carson

"Old age is like everything else. To make a success of it, you've got to start young."

Fred Astaire

"In his later years Pablo Picasso was not allowed to roam an art gallery unattended, for he had previously been discovered in the act of trying to improve on one of his old masterpieces."

Anon

"I have the body of an 18-year-old. I keep it in the fridge."

Spike Milligan

Living and Loving Life

"50 years old. In Led Zeppelin terms, that's halfway up the stairway to heaven'"

Anon

"I have found that if you love life, life will love you back."

Arthur Rubinstein

"Too many people spend money they haven't earned, to buy things they don't want, to impress people they don't like."

Will Rogers

"I feel sorry for people who don't drink. They wake up in the morning and that's the best they're going to feel all day."

Dean Martin

"I am really looking forward as I get older and older, to being less and less nice."

Annette Bening

"I'm not a heavy drinker; I can sometimes go for hours without touching a drop."

Noel Coward

"There's no reason to be the richest man in the cemetery. You can't do any business from there."

Colonel Sanders

"Twenty years from now you will be more disappointed by the things that you didn't do than by the ones you did do. So throw off the bowlines. Catch the trade winds in your sails. Explore. Dream. Discover."

Mark Twain

"Don't ask what the world needs. Ask what makes you come alive and go do it. Because what the world needs is more people who have come alive."

Howard Thurman

"A journey of a thousand miles begins with a single step."

Lao Tzu

"Retirement is wonderful. It's doing nothing without worrying about getting caught at it."

Gene Perret

"Retirement? You're talking about death, right?"

Robert Altman

"Retirement kills more people than hard work ever did."

Malcolm Forbes

"You are not in this world to live up to other people's expectations, nor should you feel the world must live up to yours."

F. Perl

"Life is either a daring adventure or nothing."

Helen Keller

"In the end, it's not going to matter how many breaths you took, but how many moments took your breath away."

Shing Xiong

"Be more concerned with your character than your reputation, because your character is what you really are, while your reputation is merely what others think you are."

John Wooden

"Money isn't everything, but it sure keeps you in touch with your children."

J. Paul Getty

"I'm living so far beyond my income that we may almost be said to be living apart."

E. E. Cummings

"For me, there are two types of people: the young and the experienced."

A. P. J. Abdul Kalam

"I exercise strong self-control. I never drink anything stronger than gin before breakfast."

W. C. Fields

"You are never too old to set another goal or to dream a new dream."

Les Brown

"From our birthday, until we die, is but the winking of an eye."

William Butler Yeats

"When a man has a birthday, he takes a day off. When a woman has a birthday, she takes at least three years off."

Joan Rivers

"My only fear is that I may live too long. This would be a subject of dread to me."

Thomas Jefferson

"My secret for staying young is good food, plenty of rest and a makeup man with a spray gun."

Bob Hope

"I have a rare intolerance which means I can only drink fermented liquids such as gin."

Julie Walters

"The secret of staying young is to live honestly, eat slowly and lie about your age."

Lucille Ball

"The old believe everything, the middle-aged suspect everything, the young know everything."

Oscar Wilde

"Hell, if I'd jumped on all the dames I'm supposed to have jumped on, I'd have had no time to go fishing."

Clark Gable

"A woman drove me to drink and I didn't even have the decency to thank her."

W. C. Fields

"The young man knows the rules, but the old man knows the exceptions."

Oliver Wendell Holmes, Sr.

"There comes a time when you should stop expecting other people to make a big deal about your birthday. That time is age 11."

Dave Barry

"Give a man a fish and he has food for a day. Teach him how to fish and you can get rid of him for the entire weekend."

Zenna Schaffer

"At my age, I want to wake up and see sunshine pouring in through the windows every day."

John Cleese

"A man can be much amused when he hears himself seriously called an old man for the first time."

T. Kinnes

"Your marriage is in trouble if your wife says, 'You're only interested in one thing,' and you can't remember what it is."

Milton Berle

"I still find each day too short for all the thoughts I want to think, all the walks I want to take, all the books I want to read, and all the friends I want to see."

John Burroughs

"Today is the yesterday you worried about tomorrow."

Anon

"Even though you're growing up, you should never stop having fun."

Nina Dobrev

"Youth would be an ideal state if it came a little later in life."

Herbert Asquith

"I am long on ideas, but short on time. I expect to live to be only about a hundred."

Thomas Edison

"To keep the heart unwrinkled, to be hopeful, kindly, cheerful, reverent – that is to triumph over old age."

Thomas B. Aldrich

"Men are like wine. Some turn to vinegar, but the best improve with age."

C. E. M. Joad

"The French are true romantics. They feel the only difference between a man of 40 and one of 70 is 30 years of experience."

Maurice Chevalier

"Ageing seems to be the only available way to live a long life."

Daniel Francois Esprit Auber

"There's one more terrifying fact about old people: I'm going to be one soon."

P. J. O'Rourke

"I can honestly say I love getting older. Then again, I never put my glasses on before looking in the mirror."

Cherie Lunghi

"As I'm getting older, I'm enjoying my vices so much more because I feel like I've deserved them."

Brooke Shields

"Male menopause is a lot more fun than female menopause. With female menopause you gain weight and get hot flashes. Male menopause – you get to date young girls and drive motorcycles."

John Wayne

"I don't plan to grow old gracefully. I plan to have facelifts until my ears meet."

Rita Rudner

"Live as if you were to die tomorrow. Learn as if you were to live forever."

Mahatma Gandhi

"No one is so old as to think he cannot live one more year."

Marcus T. Cicero

"Imperfection is beauty, madness is genius and it's better to be absolutely ridiculous than absolutely boring."

Marilyn Monroe

"Look to the future, because that is where you'll spend the rest of your life."

George Burns

"There is a very fine line between 'hobby' and 'mental illness.'"

Dave Barry

"It is better to be young in your failures than old in your successes."

Flannery O'Connor

"The best birthdays of all are those that haven't arrived yet."

Robert Orben

"Money is something you make in case you don't die."

Joseph Heller

"I'd like to grow very old as slowly as possible."

Irene Mayer Selznick

"I have spent my whole life up to a minute ago being younger than I am now."

John Ciardi

"You're only young once, but you can be immature forever."

John Grier

"Do or do not. There is no try."

Yoda

"To love oneself is the beginning of a lifelong romance."

Oscar Wilde

"All life is an experiment. The more experiments you make, the better."

Ralph Waldo Emerson

"The trouble with retirement is that you never get a day off."

Abe Lemons

Forever Young

"Life may not be the party we hoped for, but while we are here we might as well dance."

J. Williams

"I refuse to admit I'm more than 52, even if that does make my sons illegitimate."

Lady Nancy Astor

"Darling, my attitude is 'f*ck it'; I'm doing everything with everyone."

Freddie Mercury

"I don't want to retire. I'm not that good at crossword puzzles."

Norman Mailer

"The ageing process has you firmly in its grasp if you never get the urge to throw a snowball."

Doug Larson

"Nobody grows old merely by living a number of years. We grow old by deserting our ideals. Years may wrinkle the skin, but to give up enthusiasm wrinkles the soul."

Samuel Ullman

"You are as young as your faith, as old as your doubt; as young as your self-confidence, as old as your fear; as young as your hope, as old as your despair."

Douglas MacArthur

"Age does not diminish the extreme disappointment of having a scoop of ice cream fall from the cone."

Jim Fiebig

"Worrying is like a rocking chair: it gives you something to do, but it gets you nowhere."

Glenn Turner

"A kid once said to me 'Do you get hangovers?' I said, 'To get hangovers you have to stop drinking.'"

Lemmy Kilmister

"Youth is when you're allowed to stay up late on New Year's Eve. Middle age is when you're forced to."

Bill Vaughan

"Grow old along with me!
The best is yet to be,
The last of life, for which the first
was made:
Our times are in His hand
Who saith, 'A whole I planned,
Youth shows but half; trust God: see
all, nor be afraid!"

Robert Browning

"Now is the time to become a myth."

Diane Von Furstenberg

"It was one of the deadliest and heaviest feelings of my life to feel that I was no longer a boy. From that moment I began to grow old in my own esteem... and in my esteem age is not estimable."

Lord Byron

"As men get older, the toys get more expensive."

Marvin Davis

"Ageing seems to be the only available way to live a long life."

Daniel Francois Esprit Aube

"I no longer have upper arms. I have wing-span."

Bette Midler

"The afternoon knows what the morning never suspected."

Robert Frost

"Sometimes I think it would be easier to avoid old age, to die young, but then you'd never complete your life, would you? You'd never wholly know you."

Marilyn Monroe

"Another belief of mine: that everyone else my age is an adult, whereas I am merely in disguise."

Margaret Atwood

"There is a fountain of youth: It is your mind, your talents, the creativity you bring to your life and the lives of people you love. When you learn to tap this source, you will truly have defeated age."

Sophia Loren

"I'm not bald, I'm just taller than my hair."

Clive Anderson

"I am at that age. Too young for the bowling green, too old for Ecstasy."

Rab C. Nesbitt

"You don't stop laughing when you grow old, you grow old when you stop laughing."

George Bernard Shaw

"Women may be the one group that grows more radical with age."

Gloria Steinem

"It is lovely to meet an old person whose face is deeply lined, a face that has been deeply inhabited, to look in the eyes and find light there."

John O'Donohue

"As long as I am breathing, in my eyes I am just beginning."

Criss Jami

"Wisdom is the reward for surviving our own stupidity."

Brian Rathbone

"You know you're getting old when you're interested in going home before you get to where you're going."

Alan Mainwaring

"You don't realize what fine fighting material there is in old age. You show me anyone who's lived to over 70 and you show me a fighter – someone who's got the will to live."

Agatha Christie

"Buying presents for old people is a problem. I would rather like it if people came to my house and took things away."

Clement Freud

"Like many women my age, I am 28 years old."

Mary Schmitt

"It's never too late to learn some embarrassingly basic, stupidly obvious things about oneself."

Alain de Botton

"It is best as one grows older to strip oneself of possessions, to shed oneself downward like a tree, to be almost wholly earth before one dies."

Sylvia Townsend Warner

"I rented a bounce house for my adults-only 50th birthday and had a blast jumping in the stupid thing. I kept expecting the Age Police to show up and ticket me."

Janet Periat

"Middle age occurs when you are too young to take up golf and too old to rush the net."

Franklin P. Jones

"A birthday is just the first day of another 365-day journey around the sun. Enjoy the trip."

Anon

"Time is the coin of your life. It is the only coin you have, and only you can determine how it will be spent. Be careful lest you let other people spend it for you."

Carl Sandburg

"The more you praise and celebrate your life, the more there is in life to celebrate."

Oprah Winfrey

"We are only young once. That is all society can stand."

Bob Bowen

"The good old days are now."

Tom Clancy

"Anyone who stops learning is old, whether at 20 or 80. Anyone who keeps learning stays young. The greatest thing in life is to keep your mind young."

Henry Ford

"Every man over 40 is a scoundrel."

George Bernard Shaw

"Age appears to be best in four things: old wood best to burn, old wine to drink, old friends to trust, and old authors to read."

Francis Bacon

"It's not how old you are, it's how you are old."

Jules Renard

"You only live once, but if you do it right, once is enough."

Mae West

"By common consent, grey hairs are a crown of glory: the only object of respect that can never excite envy."

George Bancroft

"Some men like shiny new toys. Others like the priceless antique."

Donna Lynn Hope

"When it comes to staying young, a mindlift beats a facelift any day."

Marty Bucella

"There are three periods in life: youth, middle age and 'how well you look.'"

Nelson Rockefeller

"The tragedy of old age is not that one is old, but that one is young."

Oscar Wilde

"Regrets are the natural property of grey hairs."

Charles Dickens

"Don't be afraid your life will end; be afraid that it will never begin."

Grace Hansen

"I am old enough to see how little I have done in so much time, and how much I have to do in so little."

Sheila Kaye Smith

"My idea of hell is to be young again."

Marge Piercy

"I will never be an old man. To me, old age is always 15 years older than I am."

Bernard M. Baruch

"He who laughs, lasts."

Mary Pettibone Poole

"Always read stuff that will make you look good if you die in the middle of it."

P. J. O'Rourke

"As I grow older, I pay less attention to what men say. I just watch what they do."

Malcolm Forbes

"The whiter my hair becomes, the more ready people are to believe what I say."

Bertrand Russell

"When I was young, I was told: 'You'll see when you're 50.' I'm 50 and I haven't seen a thing."

Erik Satie

"With mirth and laughter let old wrinkles come."

William Shakespeare

"The only reason I wear glasses is for little things, like driving my car – or finding it."

Woody Allen

"I still have a full deck. I just shuffle slower."

Milton Berle

"Now I'm over 50 my doctor says I should go out and get more fresh air and exercise. I said, 'All right, I'll drive with the car window down.'"

Angus Walker

"First law on holes – when you're in one, stop digging."

Denis Healey

"Being loved keeps you young."

Madonna

"I swim a lot. It's either that or buy a new golf ball."

Bob Hope

"May you live to be 100 and may the last voice you hear be mine."

Frank Sinatra

"Be still and cool in thine own mind and spirit."

George Fox